THE BOWIE KNIFE
IN AMERICAN HISTORY
WESTERN
DE OPPRESSO LIBER
DE OPPRESSO LIBER

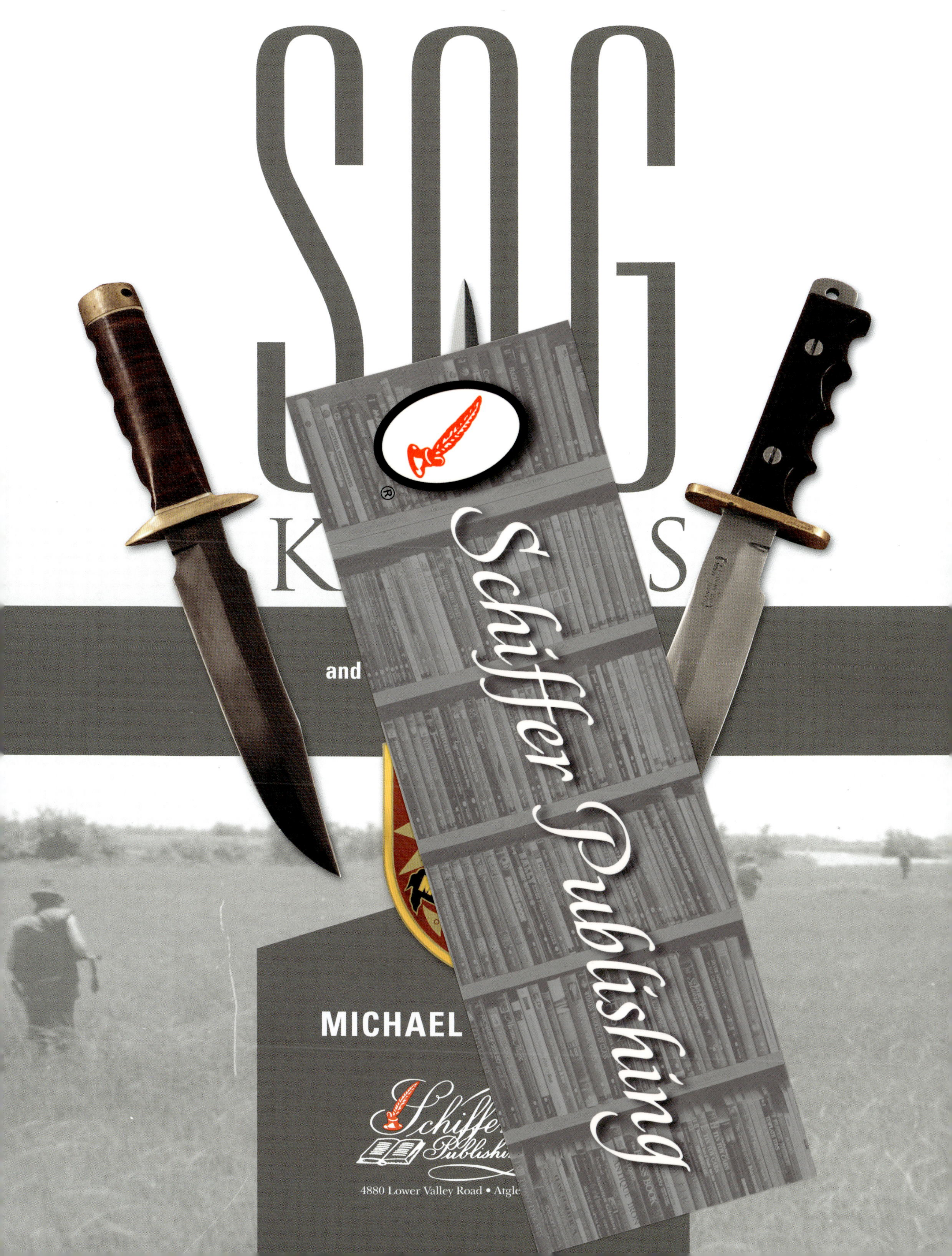

SOG®

K S

and

MICHAEL

4880 Lower Valley Road • Atgle

Schiffer Publishing

Library of Congress Control Number: 2016945357

Photography, layout, and design by Michael W. Silvey
Cover design by Justin Watkinson
Type set in Empire BT/Minion Pro

ISBN: 978-0-7643-5198-3
Printed in China

Published by Schiffer Publishing, Ltd.
4880 Lower Valley Road
Atglen, PA 19310
Phone: (610) 593-1777; Fax: (610) 593-2002
E-mail: Info@schifferbooks.com
Web: www.schifferbooks.com

To

The Oregon Posse

Who generously support our troops in faraway places

CONTENTS

ACKNOWLEDGMENTS

When you have been collecting for more than thirty years and benefitted from the help of other, more experienced collectors who have willingly given generously of their time and advice it is difficult to know where to begin thanks. I will name the people who come to mind, though I know I will forget to include someone who has contributed to my efforts and I beg forgiveness. Don Andringa, Art Moore, and Mike Squyer were the first to get me interested in knives by telling me the history of the men that made them. They identified the patterns and words like saddlehorn, whittler, sunfish, stockman, cattleman, dog leg, serpentine, jumbo, lockback, slipjoint, muscrat, peach seed, worm grove, winterbottom bone, trapper, barlow, jack, spey, canoe, and a hundred more that came to life. We spent many a pleasant hour discussing the merits of makers long gone, but there was a love for their trade and an appreciation of their craftsmanship. It was Mike Squyer who challenged me one day, sayin', "there are more than thirty variations of the US Navy Mark 1 sheath knife. It would be something to get them all." And so it was I got into military knives and expanded my circle of knife friends. There was Ernie Modlin, Fred Bratmon, M.H. (Howard) Cole, John Sabol, Gary Ruleford, Adrian VanDyk, Tom Clinton and family, John Fischer, Richard Sams, Dick Raynor, John Gibson, Gary Boyd, Rick Champlin, Miguel Hughes (who collected many of the knives herein), Garry Zalesky, Bernard Levine, Frank Trzaska, Phil Bailey, Gary Ruleford, Bill Mesquita, John Brunner, Ed Henry, Al Betters, Bill Adams, Bob Burtscher, Tony Berg, Rod Smith, Charlie Shipman, Mike Luft, Scott Moore, Arch Poeppel, Bruce Cowee, Marc Lasky, John Korompilas, Ron Flook, Bob and Pat Sullivan, Ralph Hagan, Chuck Karwan, Louis Chow, Al Hunt, John Larson, Stanley Chan, Ed Kalinowski, Steven Dick, Bill Windrum, Houston Price (of Knife World, who introduced me to publishing), Bob Lowry, Dennis and Elayne Ellingsen, Bill Walters, Mark Zalesky, Pete Hamilton, Jason Hardy, Doug Smith, Bud Morgan, and BK Brooks. I know I forgot someone and I am sorry. Thank you all for the education in cutlery and for the kindness you have shown over the years. Thanks for selling and trading knives with me. Thanks also to the book dealers and collectors who supported my work. Thanks to those who have written books and shared their knowledge—what a gift. Thanks also to my family: my wife, Ellen; daughter and proofreader, Jenn; and son and advisor, Matt.

INTRODUCTION

I grew up in 1940s and 1950s America, when the cultural standard of doing the right thing was important and generally accepted by all. Our heroes were Roy Rogers, the Lone Ranger, Superman, and others ... all icons of high moral values. Values we understood were shared by all. We believed the news and we believed the government. There was, of course, a seedier and coarser side of life, but it was kept hidden from view, and that was as it should be. The 1960s ushered in the Vietnam War and our loss of innocence; the world became a darker place. Monumental cultural and societal changes were brewing. This is the context in which I view the Vietnam era. Every time I visit that era I eke out some new understanding of how and why the world changed. I find this era endlessly fascinating, and perhaps that is why I am so attached to it as a collector of US military knives. The purpose of this book is to take a look at the most collectible and desirable knives of that war. It is primarily a book for collectors, but I am hopeful it will offer some insight into the men who walked into that battle of physical conflict and cultural change.

There were thousands of knives in the Southeast Asia theater of war. All the standard issue knives and bayonets were there, including the m4, m5, m6, and m7 bayonets, the Mark 1 utility knives of the navy, the marine corps' Ka-Bar, jet pilot survival knives, pocketknives, and machetes by the score. Most of these came out of mothballs after being put aside at the conclusions of WWII and the Korean War. Pressed back into service, they aptly filled a need. There were a few new experimental knives and, of course, a fresh bayonet for the newly adopted M16 rifle. Almost all of these knives have been the subject of observation and discourse over the years and are quite well known, requiring little further discussion. There is a group of knives, though—some surrounded in mystery, some the personal equipment of professional warriors, some originating in the jungles of Southeast Asia, and some given as presentation awards for a task well done—that are the knives we will be looking at.

In 1997, I authored *Knives of the United States Military in Vietnam*. One section in that book was about SOG knives and other blades associated with United States special forces in Southeast Asia. Another book, *SOG Knife Collector*, revisited that special area of collecting and took a fresh look at these fascinating knives. This book expands on and, in some cases, duplicates these previous studies with a focus on the knives associated with members of Military Assistance Command Vietnam Studies and Observations Group (MACV-SOG), US special forces, and other professional soldiers in Vietnam.

SOG was a clandestine army that carried on a secret war for many years and was composed of some of the best and brightest young men America had to offer. This book quite narrowly focuses on one single item of equipment these men carried and often kept as mementos of their service: their knives.

A characteristic of this study is that it explores the knives in detail. There is a greater number of photographs and some of the things previously described only by word in books or articles are now shown in photographic detail, helping the reader better understand the particular feature. These knives have become valuable assets and there are always those who attempt to dupe a potential buyer with a counterfeit specimen. The data presented here, in addition to informing the reader, may also arm the buyer against unscrupulous sellers.

In 1987, I visited the Bay Area Knife Collectors Association's annual knife show, in San Jose, California. There were several of us military knife collectors gathered around a friend's table, just chatting about knives, when we were approached by an unfamiliar face. He asked if he could show us some knives and opened his attaché case. All of us were stunned by what we saw. He had SOG knife prototypes, square and round tip bolos, and a variety of knives acquired in Southeast Asia. We learned he was Ben Baker, who had been intimately involved with the development of SOG knives and many other things related to the clandestine operations conducted by MACV-SOG. He was a deputy director of a civilian operation called the Counter Insurgency Support Office (CISO), which was charged with supplying the 5th Special Forces Group. Baker had kept excellent notes over the years and was able to document much of the history of these wonderful blades, including the dates orders were placed and received. CISO, under Baker, was responsible for a great many of the SOG knives, but there are other SOG knives whose origins and numbers remain uncertain and murky.

While there is always some danger in collecting any type of knife that you may end up with a bad one, collecting SOG knives can be an even riskier endeavor, because there are so few examples about. Included in this book are knives that I know to be good, honest specimens. I have confidence those shown herein are correct in all aspects. There are likely other knives that could have been included of which I am unaware and still others that I have seen but do not quite believe they are the real deal. As a collector, experience has shown that the more you see of the correct items you wish to collect, the easier it is to spot the phonies. This book is designed to give you sufficient information and a number of good photographs to view and study so you can identify a SOG knife.

This book also contains others knives of the period: there are Randalls, Gerbers, Eks, and others that have become quite sought after in their own right. Many of these knives have been the subject of detailed discussions and study over the years and they can be viewed here as an introduction and, perhaps, an appetizer to new areas of collecting.

Good luck with your collecting.

Yours truly,
Michael W. Silvey

SOG KNIVES

Even the name is fascinating: Military Assistance Command Vietnam - Studies and Observations Group. It perhaps brings to mind a group of social scientists or bespectacled explorers in khaki shorts and pith helmets with butterfly nets. On the contrary MACV-SOG was an unconventional warfare task force engaged in highly classified clandestine (dark) operations throughout Southeast Asia. It was a secret, multi-service United States special operations unit that conducted covert unconventional warfare operations prior to and during the Vietnam War. In 1963, the Vietnamese Special Forces Command was established and their operations were supported and financed by the United States Central Intelligence Agency. In 1964, the government of South Vietnam created the Special Exploitation Service to take over these operations. At the same time, MACV-SOG was established to take over the CIA's job of assisting, advising, and supporting the new organization in secret sabotage, psychological, and special operations in North and South Vietnam, Laos, Cambodia, and southern China. MACV-SOG also captured enemy prisoners, rescued downed pilots, and retrieved US personnel who were held prisoner throughout Southeast Asia, as well as conducted agent team activities. MACV-SOG was created in January 1964, and was primarily comprised of personnel from the US Army Special Forces, US Navy SEALs, US Air Force, and the CIA, as well as some elements of the USMC Force Recon units. The United States Counter Insurgency Support Office (CISO) in Okinawa provided logistical support for these special forces programs. In 1963, Ben Baker was deputy chief of CISO; when SOG was created in 1964, he helped provide special forces the materials and supplies they needed for their operations.

Baker was a man who had been in the field and paid attention to detail, yet was pragmatic, practical, and dedicated to getting the job done. When he took on the task of providing knives for special forces and SOG, he tested a variety of steels for suitability, then worked on blade and handle designs. He credits his handle design to his old Marble's Woodcrafter skinning/hunting knife. Indeed, the stacked leather washer handle, threaded tang, and pommel nut are quite similar. The blade designs are unique, but bear resemblance to classic American Bowie designs. CISO worked through trading companies for many of the products that were required, and this was the case when it came to knives. The Yogi Shokai Company of Naha, Okinawa, was the trading company that provided knives, among other items, to CISO. Like a broker, Yogi Shokai contracted with cutlery firms for the knives and the maker's identity was not passed on to CISO and probably will never be known for certain. Most likely the knives were made in Japan and the names of Japan Sword and Kiffe have been offered as possible sources. The steel used in the blades was identified by the supplier as SKS 3, which in addition to iron specs out with the following elements included: C = 0.9 - 1.0, Si - less 0.35, Mn = 0.9 - 1.2, P = less 0.03, S = less 0.03, Cr = .05 - 1.0, and W = 0.5 - 1.0.

The CISO SOG knives were delivered beginning in June 1964. The first batch contained 1,300 seven-inch knives, plus eight prototypes. The unit cost was $9.85. Most of these seven-inch knives went to cross border recon teams and saw rough service. The jungle has a way of accelerating decay and many of the knives did not make it back in good condition—some never came back at all. These seven-inch recon knives are now some of the rarest and most sought after of all US military issue knives. The next batch of knives was received by CISO in October 1966. These had six-inch blue blades and a rather bulbous-shaped guard, hence the collectors' nickname, "fat guard SOG." The next deliveries took place between March and August 1967 and the blades were numbered 1 through 3700. The number was etched on the ricasso on the back side of the blade. A portion of these numbered knives were delivered with blue blades—typically those with numbers under 1000. Later deliveries had plum-colored blades. Exactly where the split between blue and plum takes place is uncertain, but I have seen an 813 that is blue and a number 915 that is plum-colored and a number 986 that is back to blue. It was reported that the first batch of knives were not properly heat treated and were returned. Evidently, they were disassembled and run through the heat treat process again. Those undergoing this procedure ended up with blue blades. Subsequent blades were plum-colored. The unit cost of these six-inch knives was $8.40.

There is another batch of some 1,700 plum SOG knives that were ordered through CISO for the 5th Special Forces Mess Association. These knives are identical to the numbered versions but are marked with the special forces crest and the inscription, "5th Special Forces Group (Abn)/Vietnam." These knives were given as presentation pieces and as end-of-tour mementos. It was fairly common for any variety of SOG knife to be engraved, personalized, and given as a presentation. All SOG knives came with a well-made black leather sheath with a two-grit stone in a pocket attached to the sheath front.

There are a variety of other SOG knives that came out of Vietnam but their origin is clouded. One of these is the Iron Guard SOG. The profile lines of this blade are somewhat more exaggerated than those of the CISO SOGs. The fit and finish is also of a lower quality. The guard and pommel are of iron, and are often found with a reddish tint. This knife was supplied with a well-made black leather sheath with a stone pocket. Sometimes these knives were chrome or nickle plated and/or engraved for presentation.

A variation almost identical in profile to the CISO knife has brass or iron fittings that have been lacquered a bluish green color. The knives of this variation have the number 5000 stamped into the ricasso on the obverse of the blade. The sheaths are nearly identical to those issued with the CISO SOGs. It has been reported that these were procured by the CIA's liaison officers for distribution to the command and control compound's supply office. The blades are a most unusual bright blue color and the pommel has a serial number stamped into it.

All of the SOG knives observed have spacers in the handle. Most are white plastic or nylon type material, as opposed to the vulcanized fiber used by knife makers in this country. Except where noted, the spacers are at either end of the leather washer handle and are used to separate the leather from the guard and pommel. The iron guard knives with exaggerated blade profiles usually have black fiber spacers next to the guard and pommel. With regard to guards and pommels, all observed have been cast, not fabricated from solid stock. Most custom makers solder the guards to the blade, but this is not the case with commercially made knives like the SOGs. Finally, I have noticed at least four variations of SOG sheaths.

The SOG knives were born out of and for secret operations, and much mystery will forever surround them. Even the Americans who were part of the mobile launch teams, mobile strike forces, forward operations bases, recon teams, and the projects seldom discuss their assignments with others, perhaps out of habit, but also because much of what took place was and may remain classified. Perhaps it is because of this mystique that these knives are a favorite area of collecting for many.

This section focuses on a very narrow area of collecting. In this study we look at SOG knives and a few others associated with SOG. So what is a SOG knife? The photographs and captions on the following pages will provide a glimpse of several varieties of these knives. A more detailed look at these knives will provide the reader with an answer to this question.

1
2
3
4
5
6
7
8
9
10
11
12
13
14
15
16
17
18
19
20

SOG Knives from the Previous Page

1. CISO Plum Presentation. Standard inscription on the reverse side of the blade showing the special gorces crest on the ricasso, along with "5th SPECIAL FORCES GROUP (Abn)/VIETNAM." It should be noted that some of these plum SOG colors can vary from a bright reddish color to a dark reddish brown or maroon.
2. Sterile Iron Guard. Blue blade. Iron fittings are sometimes red tinted.
3. CISO Fat Guard. The first batch of six-inch SOG knives were this variety.
4. CISO Plum #1710. Numbers are on the reverse of the blade.
5. CISO Blue Blade #813. By way of explanation, I have heard some of the numbered CISO SOG knives were not of appropriate hardness and were re-hardened. Those that were have blue blades (a mix of blues to almost a Parkerized finish). Generally, those below about #900 were blue while those above were plum.
6. CISO Fat Guard.
7. CISO Fat Guard.
8. CISO Fat Guard.
9. Presentation SOG with iron fittings. Standard presentation and inscription showing the special forces crest on the ricasso, reverse side of the blade, and "5th SPECIAL FORCES GROUP (Abn)/VIETNAM."
10. Sterile Iron Guard.
11. CISO Fat Guard with personalized presentation, "PRESENTED TO MARK ROCK/FOR OUTSTANDING SERVICE/VIETNAM 28 NOV 70 – 1 NOV 71." No rank shown, so probably a civilian.
12. Early CISO Fat Guard. Note the black spacers and exaggerated grind lines. This was the very first of the six-inch knives to be delivered to CISO. The blade is blue with red around the edges.
13. CISO Plum #2211.
14. CISO Plum #3494.
15. Presentation SOG with aluminum fittings. Standard presentation and inscription showing the Special Forces crest on the ricasso, reverse side of the blade, and "5th SPECIAL FORCES GROUP (Abn)/VIETNAM."
16. CISO Plum completely unmarked and sterile. The only one of these I have encountered.
17. CISO Plum #1922.
18. Presentation SOG with aluminum fittings. Standard presentation and inscription showing the special forces crest on the ricasso, reverse side of the blade, and "5th SPECIAL FORCES GROUP (Abn)/VIETNAM."
19. The first of the CISO SOG knives, the Seven-Inch SOG Recon.
20. The first of the CISO SOG knives, the Seven-Inch SOG Recon.

THE SEVEN-INCH SOG RECON

Some 1,300 of these Seven-Inch SOG Recon knives were ordered by the US Army Counter Insurgency Support Office (CISO) in June 1964. The cost was $9.85 each. At about this time, United States Military Assistance Command Vietnam assumed some of the duties previously under the direction of the United States Central Intelligence Agency.

The knife on the previous page was found in a batch of army surplus uniforms and gear after the lot had been sold in the San Francisco Bay area in the 1980s. It has seen plenty of heavy use. Contrast this with the knife in the following photo that has seen little use. Construction of these knives is quite good. The fittings are of chemically blackened cast brass. The pommels are not solid—mostly hollow—and show evidence of casting. The guard was cast to accept a wider ricasso that resulted from a change during the original evaluation of the knife. The choil area was relieved to allow a user to get his fingers around the front side of the guard, enhancing pull and leverage when extracting a blade. This left a slight recess in the guard below the blade. I have never seen an issued Seven-Inch CISO Recon that did not have this characteristic.

The above knife came out of an estate sale and when it was obtained, it was still covered with jungle mud and crud but was surprisingly intact. It is missing the flap for the stone pocket, but all else is there, including a very rare original sharpening stone. The knife below came from an air force master sergeant who worked in Project Ranch Hand out of Ton Son Nhut Air Base, Saigon. This project was designed to deny the enemy the cover of the jungle by removing it and they did so by spraying Agent Orange in great quantities over the jungle. Their motto: "Only you can prevent a forest." Agent Orange was later found to cause a great number of serious health problems for those who worked in the program.

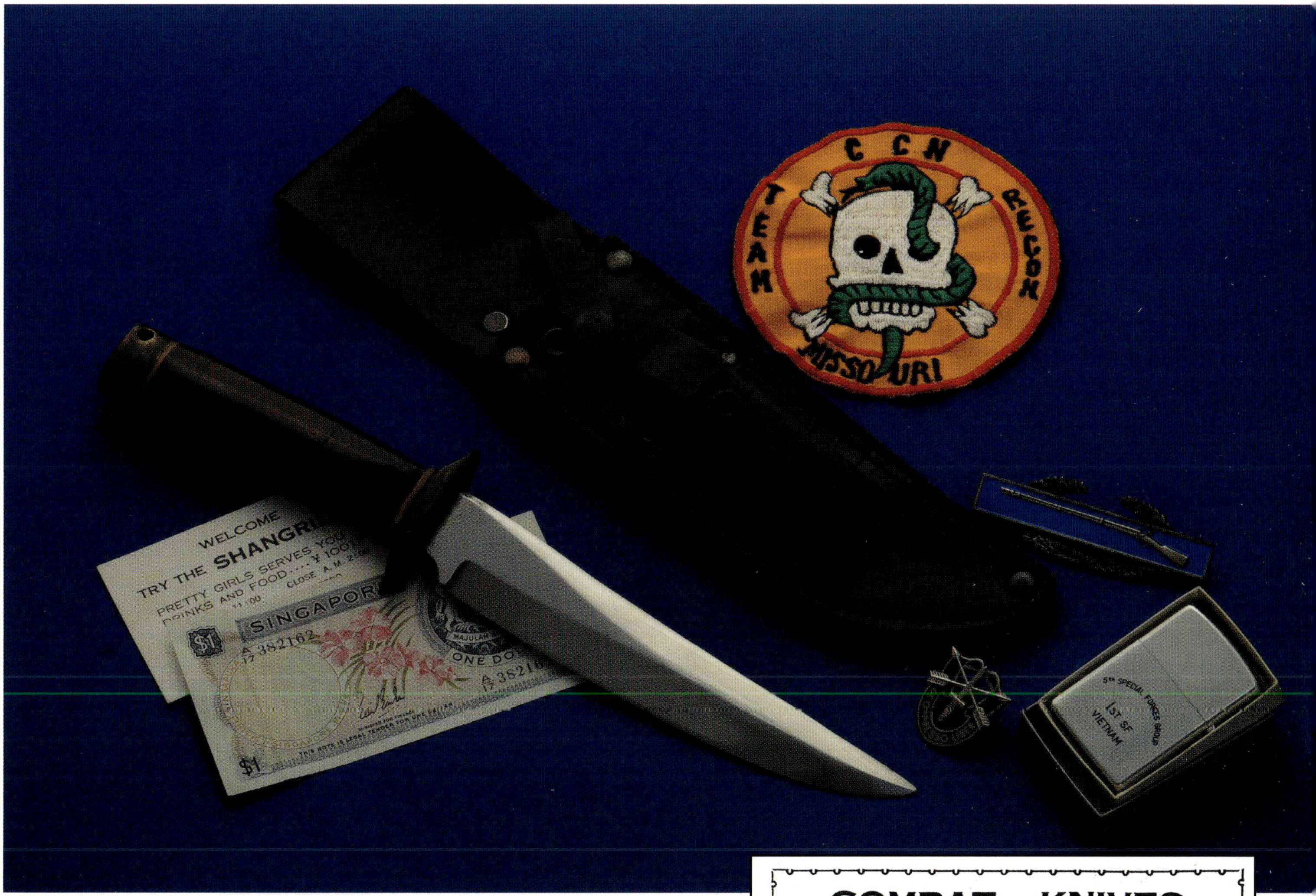

This CISO SOG knife is paired with a sheath normally found with the Sterile Iron Guard SOG, which has a six-inch blade. The scabbard is roomy enough to accommodate this seven-inch blade. The blade thickness on these knives measured at the ricasso varies from knife to knife, ranging from about 0.242 to 0.270 inches.

COMBAT KNIVES

For Free-World Forces
by Japan Sword Co., Ltd.

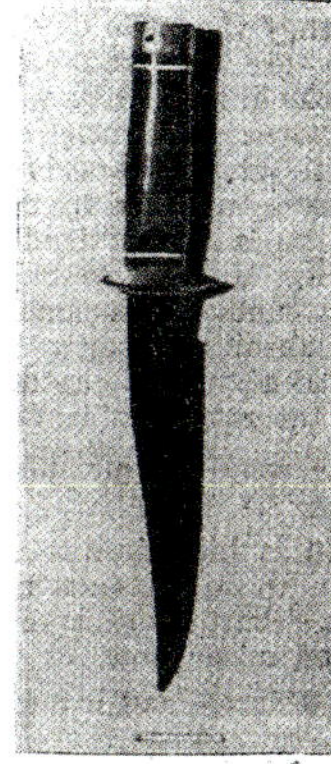

The samurai warriors of ancient Japan regarded their swords as the very essence of their profession of arms and the blade attained almost the same status as the cross to Christians.

The art of making swords in Japan became a guarded technique handed down from father to son during the feudal era in Japan.

Today, Japan sword company offers products that are the result of this tradition. Forging and tempering of each blade is actually done by hand.

The Japan Sword Company today is headed by Inami Hajusui, a well known expert on Japanese Swords and the lineal descendant of a family devoted to swordmaking (Katana) since the 17th Century.

NOW AVAILABLE AT $20, for the first time.
Model # 780, Overall Length 12 inches
Blade length 7 inches

Black combat finished, hand-forged carbon steel. Rawhide handle, with solid brass fittings.
Complete with scabbard.
Mail this coupon, with $20 check, or money order.

To : **Asian Discount Sales, P.O. Box 15044, HONGKONG.**
Please rush me . . . . . . COMBAT KNIVES, (remittance enclosed). My address is :
Name : . . . . **Serial #** . . . .
Unit : . . . .
Address : . . . . **APO SF** . . . .

CIA KNIFE

In the past, the seven-inch knife shown opposite and on the following page was thought to be associated with the CIA or SOG. One could imagine the knife—made by Japan Sword—having been carried by some members of SOG, though it was not an issue item; rather, it was available by private purchase, as documented by the advertisement shown. This ad was found in an English language news magazine titled *Life in Vietnam*, No. 117, dated June 17, 1967.

It is unknown how many of these knives were sold as a result of this and other ads like it, but few are found by collectors and those in collections are highly prized. A six-inch version of this knife was also available.

This is the seven-inch version of the so-called "CIA knife" made by Japan Sword shown in the advertisement on the preceding page. The blade on this specimen had a blued finish.

A retired CIA operative brought this knife back from Vietnam. It was recognized by Ben Baker of CISO as one of a few prototypes provided during the process of selecting the seven-inch recon knife. On the reverse of the keeper strap are Asian characters indicating the blade should have a bright finish.

The knife below is owned by Ben Baker and is one of the trial pieces submitted during the selection process. Its design is very similar to the final issue knife shown on the preceding pages and may have been the prototype for those knives.

THE SIX-INCH CISO SOG KNIFE

FAT GUARD

In October 1966, an order was placed for the first 1,200 six-inch knives. The unit price of these knives was $8.40. This model has come to be known among collectors as the "fat guard," because of its rather bulbous guard. The first batch of these had black spacers and somewhat exaggerated grind lines, as well as an occasional red coloration to the normally blue blade. You will notice a much deeper cutout at the top of the blade just in front of the guard. These are very distinctive knives, with a profile quite different from the subsequent batch of fat guards.

This black spacer six-inch CISO fat guard was, at one time, presented to Maj. Gen. Chirapongse, commander of Thailand's elite fighting force, Division 9.

At some point in the production of the fat guard SOGs, the blade grind became a bit less dramatic and the black spacers gave way to white ones. The knives shown on the previous pages are quite rare. The second generation fat guard shown here is marked "SEA COMMANDO." The Sea Commandos were the elite fighting force of the South Vietnamese Navy, the Vietnamese equivalent of our Navy SEALs.

Maj. Ralph Gilmore served two tours of duty in Vietnam, both with special forces; he was presented with these two six-inch CISO fat guard SOG knives. He was also presented with a bolo that is shown later in this book.

SOG knives were dressed up in a number of ways and given as gifts to recognize a member's service. A recurring theme found on many of these knives and plaques is that of the "Spy vs. Spy" character of *Mad* magazine. Undoubtedly favored because of the clandestine nature of the work, "spooky" is often found on plaques, knives, bolos, and even cigarette lighters of the men who served in SOG.

The knives that CISO purchased for the US' covert war were provided by Yogi Shokai, a trading company based in Naha, Okinawa. Although we know the knives came from the Yogi Shokai Company, we do not know who the manufacturers were. It is likely one or more of the large cutlery firms in Japan were the primary contractors. Some similarity between the commercial knives marked "Japan Sword" and these fat guard SOG knives can be seen. The knife above is the standard six-inch fat guard CISO SOG knife. It no longer has the black spacers and the more radical profile of the early version. The same can be said of the knife below.

Presentations to servicemen typically include their rank along with their name. This one, which does not, leads to speculation that Mark Rock was a civilian, perhaps an employee of the Central Intelligence Agency. This particular knife, which shows some light use, was still in its original thin cardboard box when acquired. The odd folding knife at the right in the photo is an experimental knife made for use with explosives. These demolition knives were made by Camillus Cutlery Co. and less than 200 units were produced.

This is another fat guard knife used for a presentation piece. It is engraved; "PRESENTED TO/SFC WAINWRIGHT F. COX/247 46 5115." It is displayed here along with a plaque and his Special Forces green beret with the patch of Recon Team Fork.

In March 1967, CISO began to order additional knives and by November 1967, they had ordered 5,400 knives. These were a sleeker version dressed with a new, slimmer guard. The guard was pointed on each end with the idea that it made it more difficult for someone to take it out of your hand. Of the 5,400 knives, 1,700 went to the Special Forces Mess Association. These were inscribed with the special forces crest and the words "5th Special Forces Group (Abn)/ Vietnam." These knives were to be presented as mementos to members who completed their tour of duty and were heading to a new assignment. The other 3,700 knives were etched with a serial number on the reverse ricasso. There are some differences among the blades, adding a bit of interest. A portion of the first 900 to 1,000 of these blades were blue. It was not the polished blue of the fat guard model, but a rougher blue finish. There was a problem with the blade hardness and some of the early ones had to be re-done. Those coming in after number 900 or so had a nice polished finish, but the bluing process produced blades colored from red to brown. It has been reported this was a result of a different temperature of the bluing salts, but has not been verified. Whatever the cause, it made for a spectacular looking and very distinctive knife. There is also a story that the first 200 of these knives disappeared in transit (those in the 1 to 200 number range). These were reportedly replaced.

This is one of the early second model CISO SOG knives. This one is numbered 885 and has a blue blade. It is new in the box, complete with blade cover, wrap, and sheath. The handle was installed upside down. Perhaps that is why it was never issued and used. The fact that one is found in this configuration supports the idea that some of these were taken apart, re-heat treated, and then reassembled. This one may have had its handle turned around when it was reinstalled.

This is number 986, just like it came out of the box. The finish on the blade is blue like others in this category, but it should be noted there is little consistency in the finish on these blue blades: some blades are rather spotty and rough, while others are smooth and shiny.

This blue blade second model six-inch CISO SOG is numbered 613.

This six-inch CISO SOG knife (numbered 572) displays evidence it has seen some honest use. The leather shows a few wrinkles and the blade shows sharpening of the cutting and the false edges. Despite its usage it is in solid condition. The plaque piece came from SFC Kenneth Ross of CCC.

The second model six-inch CISO SOG knife shown at the top of this page is number 813 and has a blue blade. The knife below it is the same model, but is numbered 1922, and has an almost red blade. It has been observed that blades made later in the contract period (those with higher numbers) had blades that were darker—some of these were almost brown.

This knife displays a bright plum-colored blade and is numbered 2211. The numbers are not stamped into the blade; rather, they are electro-etched. The numbers stand about 3⁄16 inch tall and are in a rather bold font. Note this knife is in a scabbard typically associated with the Sterile Iron Guard knives. These knives are also found in the sheaths that usually accompany the Presentation SOGs. It is not unusual to find this knife in any of the three sheaths associated with the six-inch SOG models. It leads one to speculate that knives and sheaths were kept separately in the supply rooms and were matched up when issued. This phenomenon exists so frequently that it can't be blamed on collectors who may have inadvertently swapped sheaths.

This dark plum-colored blade is number 3490, one of the last few made. This one has a presentation-type scabbard.

This knife (number 3669) is one of the last CISO SOG knives made. When CISO was first requested to supply knives they found everyone wanted something different. Requests ranged from small hunting type knives to swords. CISO finally opted for a knife that was distinctive and unique, but most of all had a quality that would enhance the *esprit de corps* of the receiving units.

This knives shown below are second model six-inch CISO presentation SOG knives. These knives were obtained by CISO, but paid for by the Special Forces Mess Association. There were 1,700 of these made and all were electro-etched with the special forces crest and the inscription "5th SPECIAL FORCES GROUP (Abn)/VIETNAM." The etching was done prior to the coloration of the blade.

The beret shown above was worn by Chet Moore, an air force dog handler assigned to the marine corps. He and his dog, Khan, walked point for the Marines around the Da Nang area on many occasions in 1968.

This is one of 1,700 CISO SOG presentation knives purchased in May and November 1967 by the Special Forces Mess Association. Etched into the blade is the special forces crest and inscription.

The Plum Sterile Variation

Normally, the reverse side of the plum SOG blade displays the etched serial number or the 5th Special Forces Group (Abn) presentation. The knife shown shows neither. The front side of the blade shown on the previous page is also unmarked. At one time, it was believed this was just a production anomaly and the numbering was overlooked. Even as rare as they are, they seem to occur too frequently for this to be the case.

Another sterile six-inch CISO SOG Knife.

THE STERILE IRON GUARD SOG

What we have seen so far is a representation of the knives obtained by the Counter Insurgency Support Office as part of its effort to supply SOG and special forces in Southeast Asia. There is another series of knives associated with SOG, the Sterile Iron Guard model shown below. Note the similarity of the blade profile to that of the early first model black spacer CISO six-inch knife.

These knives were the property of Phillip Rice of the 46th Special Forces Group (Abn), Thailand. The MACV-SOG plaque piece, along with the plated sterile iron guard SOG knife and the presentation plate, were at one time affixed to a wooden plaque that unfortunately found favor with some very hungry termites. The blued version of this knife was issued to Staff Sgt. Rice. Official military honors and awards were somewhat discouraged for men assigned to SOG because of the covert nature of their operations. Their service was often recognized by the men they served with by the gift of a presentation plaque or knife. Phillip Rice was also a member of Recon Team Iowa in 1969.

Where this model knife originated, who ordered it, and who distributed are unknown, but it must have been made in fairly good numbers, because it is known to exist in many collections. The similarity of the fittings to others found on knives marked "Kiffe/Japan" leads one to believe these may have been made by the same manufacturer. The similarity of the blade shape of this knife to the first model six-inch CISO knife, as well as the use of black spacers, makes one suspect there could be some connection at the design stage. The fit and finish of the knife and the leather sheath of these Iron Guard models does not quite match the standard found on the CISO SOGs. Occasionally, you will see these knives engraved and given as presentation pieces. In addition, examples have been noted that were nickel or chrome plated and/or engraved as presentation gifts.

THE PRESENTATION SOG KNIVES

The following knives were made as presentation items, typically given when a man completed his tour of duty. It is unknown where these knives originated, perhaps with a mess association or an enlisted club. There are at least two versions of the knife: one has good cast iron fittings with a clear lacquer finish and the other version has aluminum fittings. There also may have been a model with brass fittings, but none were available for examination. The knives appear to have been made by the same manufacturer. Blade profiles and grind lines are the same, as well as blade thickness, with both varieties measuring 0.285 to 0.295 inches when measured at the ricasso.

The previous knife shows the aluminum fittings, while this knife displays cast iron fittings. Both specimens are with their correct scabbards, though the straight side sheath above is most often found with the Sterile Iron Guard knife.

This is a standard presentation SOG knife with aluminum fittings and regular inscription, but also bears the name of the recipient, "MSG HENRY CARDINAL." The leather wrist thong has been re-deployed as a safety keeper for use during a parachute jump.

This series of presentation SOG knives is made from stout material, with the thickness of the blade stock measuring 0.285 to 0.295 inches—nearly 5⁄16 of an inch thick. The blades in this series were blue, but they are often encountered with highlights of red, making a very attractive and distinctive blade. These blades are etched with the special forces emblem and the standard inscription, "5th SPECIAL FORCES GROUP (Abn)/VIETNAM." These knives have also been observed with the inscription that omitted the word "VIETNAM" and were reportedly given to troops who served in Laos and Cambodia. Only one of these knives has been examined and it was determined to be counterfeit.

THE 5000 SERIES SOG KNIFE

This is a very rare 5000 Series SOG Knife that has brass fittings. Most were equipped with iron guards and pommels. Those with iron fittings had the pommel hand-stamped with a four-digit serial number in the 5000 range. The sheath is nearly identical to the CISO six-inch sheath, Type III.

The 5000 series of SOG knives is quite uncommon. These are nearly identical in profile to the plum SOGs, except the fittings on most are iron castings and have been painted with a blue green lacquer finish. The ricasso on each specimen is stamped 5000, but each has a four-digit serial number in the 5000 range hand-stamped into the pommel.

This group of knives was not provided by CISO. It has been reported they were obtained by the CIA and provided to unit supply offices. Like the other SOGs, some of these have been used as presentation knives. This variety is generally more scarce than other models and most specimens show hard usage, like the knife pictured below.

At one time it was assumed these knives were made by the same manufacturer that made the CISO SOG knives because of the similarity of their profiles. Under closer examination, it becomes apparent there are differences in construction. While the pommel nut on the plum SOG is 6 × 1 mm, the nut on the 5000 series is 5 × 0.9 mm—not a standard manufactured size. Not only that, the construction of the threaded end is done differently. The Plum blade knife uses a keyhole cut into the tang that has a 6 × 1 mm machine screw brazed into the hole. The threaded end of the 5000 series blade is an integral part of the tang. A measurement of the guard and pommel show only nominal differences.

The knife shown in the inset (below) is a near mint example of the 5000 series and shows the unusual but attractive bluing done to the blades of these knives. The iron guard and pommel on this piece have been stripped of their original protective greenish-blue lacquer.

SOME OTHERS

"In Appreciation/Sgt Larry G. Purvis/Special Mission Force" is the presentation on this well used SOG knife. Special Mission Force (SMF) was part of Strategic Technical Directorate Assistance Team 158, which was the successor to SOG. SMF performed crash site and personnel recovery missions until the end of the war. Prior to that, Sgt. Purvis was part of Recon Team Iowa. This most unusual SOG knife has many of the characteristics of the 5000 series but is not numbered.

The knife in the shadow box (below) appears to be a second model six-inch CISO SOG knife that has been chrome plated as a presentation to a naval officer. Note the very unusual keeper straps for the knife and sharpening stone.

The knife on the right is also unusual, in that it is the same pattern as the second model six-inch CISO SOG knife but is unmarked, has a blue blade, and aluminum fittings. It is the only one of these models that has been encountered.

The presentation on the plaque at the left reads, "PRESENTED TO/LCDR PATRICK J. HEPHNER/COMPTROLLER STADT-158/ VIETNAM 72 - 73."

Perhaps one of the most unusual SOG knives encountered is the one (below) with cast aluminum fittings. It has a finely ground blade that is expertly blued and displays a variety of colors from red to blue. The knife and sheath, manufactured in Southeast Asia, are ringers for the CISO plum models, but it is a unique product. This knife is also shown on the previous page.

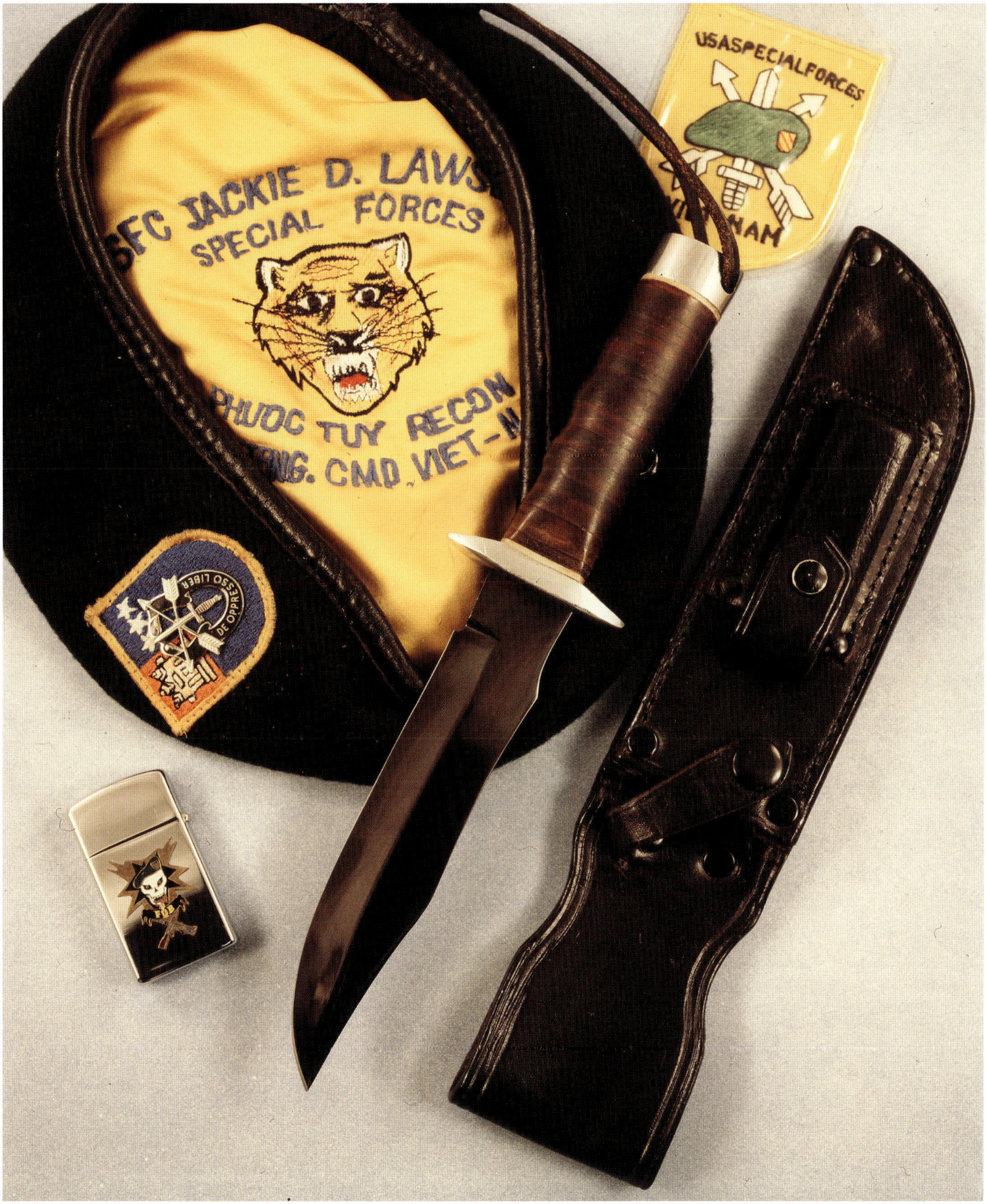

SOG KNIFE ORIGINS, MAKERS, AND QUANTITIES

Over the years, a number of SOG knives have been observed and it is with a high degree of confidence that those shown on these pages are authentic and legitimate types. The origin of some of the various models is known thanks entirely to Ben Baker (formerly of CISO), but the history of other models is clouded at best. For example, it has been found that the fittings on the Sterile Iron Guard model exactly match up with a commercial offering by Kiffe Company of New York. It may well be that Kiffe, which was not a manufacturer, bought these knives from the manufacturer of the Sterile Iron Guard SOG for re-sale in surplus stores or other outlets where an inexpensive knife would do well. It has not been possible to contact Kiffe to confirm what actually took place so the origin of this knife is unknown. Likewise, the same is true of many of the models shown in the summary below.

SOG KNIFE MODEL	LIKELY SUPPLIER	DATE	QUANTITY
Seven-Inch Recon	CISO	June, 1964	1300
Black Spacer Fat Guard	CISO	October, 1966	unknown/rare
White Spacer Fat Guard	CISO	October, 1966	1300 includes the black spacer version
Numbered Blue/Plum	CISO	March, 1967 to August, 1967	3700
Plum Sterile	CISO	March, 1967 to August, 1968	unknown
Iron Guard Sterile	unknown	unknown	unknown
Plum Presentation	CISO	May, 1967 to November, 1967	1700
Aluminum Fittings Blue	unknown	unknown	unknown but a very small quantity
Aluminum Fittings Presentation	Mess Association	unknown	unknown
Aluminum Fittings Presentation Without "Vietnam"	unknown	unknown	unknown *only one observed was a fake.
Iron Fittings Presentation	Mess Association	unknown	unknown
5000 Series Iron Fittings	CIA	unknown	unknown but likely a small number
5000 Series Brass Fittings	CIA	unknown	unknown but a very small number

MORE SOG KNIFE DETAILS

SOG SHEATHS

In his book *Knives of the U.S. Special Forces*, Tom Clinton identified four types of SOG sheaths. His Type IV sheath is the one typically found on the Seven-Inch SOG Recon. His Type III is the one most often found on the Iron and Aluminum Guard Presentation models. His Type II is the sheath associated most frequently with the Six-Inch CISO SOG knives. Finally, his Type I sheath is most often found on the Sterile Iron Guard model. There is no ironclad rule that states a particular sheath must go with a certain model SOG knife. It is evident the sheaths got mixed and matched in supply rooms, in the field, by collectors, or even all three. In any event, it is quite common to find any type of SOG knife in any of the four sheath types.

Below is a representative seven-inch CISO SOG sheath (Type IV). The leather on these is a six or seven ounce weight—rather flimsy for a knife like the seven-inch recon. The keeper strap is an extension of the welt and has a snap with a plastic cover. The plastic covered snap is also found on sheaths for the CISO six-inch and presentation models. This plastic snap is a rather unique feature difficult to duplicate on a counterfeit sheath. Most such makers just paint the snap with black enamel. It appears the seven-inch sheaths were not sealed after being dyed and normal wear and tear quickly removed some of the color, especially in the wet conditions of the jungle. The owner of this knife re-dyed the front of it. Also, note the drain hole in the lower portion of the sheath for the seven-inch SOG. On many examples this hole is only present on the front side.

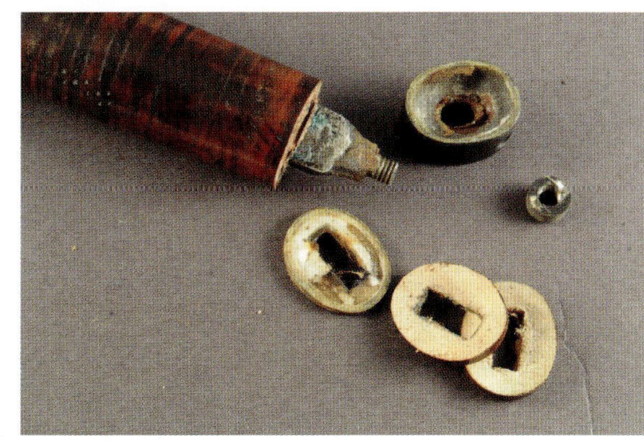

The pommel screw on the knife examined is part of the tang. The workmanship is not up to the standards found on the CISO six-inch SOGs. The pommel is cast brass and nearly identical to those found on other varieties.

SEVEN-INCH CISO SOG RECON GUARD

The photograph at the right shows the area of the guard that has been recessed for the blade to drop into. Note it extends below the lower edge of the ricasso and is an identifying feature of the authentic seven-inch CISO SOG Recon. These guards were castings, and the small area is a bit rough and shows evidence of being cast. Such details about the construction of the knife the collector should know.

This photo (left) of the snap on the keeper strap shows its inside markings. Although plastic coated snaps are used on the seven-inch recon, the CISO six-inch SOGs and Presentation sheaths have their own distinctive markings on the inside of the female portion of their snaps. The male portions all have a series of dimples around the base of the snap. Dimple count on the seven-inch snap is thirty-six. The small glove snap on the stone pocket is unmarked except for decorative dimples.

Originally, only the top grain and sides of the sheath were dyed.

THE SIX-INCH CISO SOG

The CISO six-inch SOG sheath (Type III) shows an improvement in quality over the seven-inch version. The leather thickness is a seven or eight ounce weight, the stitching is straighter, and the construction is much more professional. The snap on the stone pocket is a typical glove snap and is unmarked, but the snap on the keeper strap is plastic coated. The rivets used on these sheaths are painted black and are the compression type, composed of two parts hammered together. The leather is dyed on the top grain and edges only. The bottom grain is undyed and on some sheaths may be difficult to determine because of age and discoloration.

The markings inside the snap on the sheath keeper strap look like "(star) H K (star) T"; the meaning of these characters is not known, but knowing what they look like may be helpful for comparison.

The glove snap used on the stone pocket cover is unmarked, except for the dimples around the base of the male portion. These may be for decoration, or to improve adherence of the snap to the leather.

The construction of SOG knives is quite similar: guards and pommels are made of brass, iron, and aluminum, and all are castings. Little material was wasted on the pommel and you can see how it is hollowed out. Some of the leather spacers on this CISO SOG were removed so you could see how the knife was made. The blade had a keyhole cut into the tang. A 6 × 1 mm machine screw was fitted into the key hole, then brass was brazed in place and dressed squarely. This construction differs from the seven-inch SOG Recon knife, the 5000 series SOG, and the Sterile Iron Guard.

PRESENTATION SOG

The sheath for the Presentation SOG (Type II) is of excellent construction and made of substantial leather; it resembles the CISO sheath in many ways. The keeper strap snap is plastic covered, but is marked differently than that found on the CISO SOG sheath. Both sheaths come with identical greenish-grey two-tone sharpening stones.

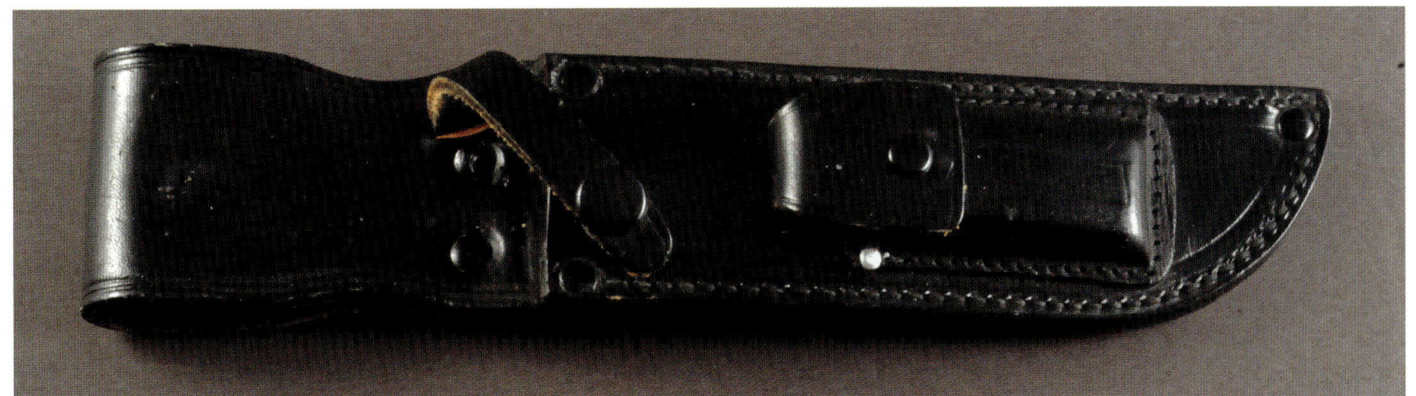

The snap on the presentation sheath is marked with Asian characters and two stars. The male portion of the snap is dimpled around the base and appears similar to that found on the CISO sheath, but differs, in that this has thirty-two dimples and the CISO has forty. The small snap on the stone pocket is marked "(star) HASI (star) HATO." The rivets at the top of the stone pocket are found bright and painted black. All leather—top, bottom, and sides—has been dyed.

The pommel arrangement on the Presentation SOG appears to be like those on the CISO seven-inch SOG recon knife. The tang was ground down and threaded to a 6 × 1 mm pattern. Whether the fittings are iron or aluminum, they are cast in the same fashion as those on the CISO SOGs.

THE IRON GUARD STERILE SOG KNIFE

The Sterile Iron Guard SOG knife scabbard (Type I) is of a quality not quite equal to that of the six-inch SOG variety sheaths; nonetheless, it is a suitable product. The rivets and snaps are chemically darkened and there are no plastic coated snaps. The leather on the back of the sheath typically shows sewing machine feed marks. The inside of the snap is marked "SWALLOW (star)." The base of the male snap is marked with thirty-two dimples.

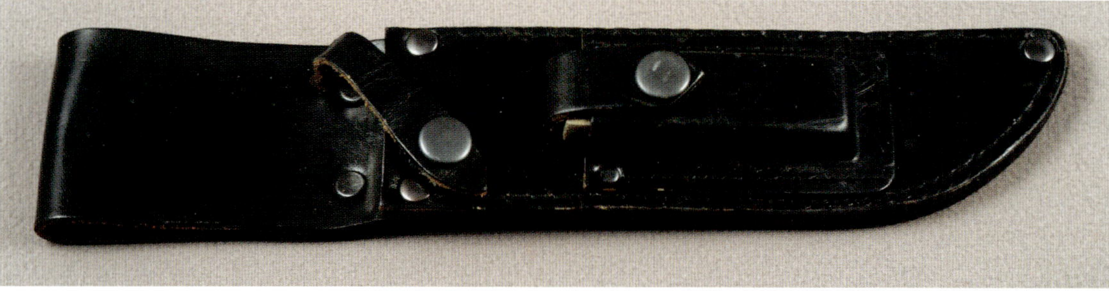

The male portion of the snaps is dimpled in the same manner as those found on the other SOG sheaths, but the entire snap has been chemically blackened. Like the Presentation SOG sheath, all leather surfaces have been dyed.

The construction of the pommel on the Iron Guard knife is nearly identical to that found on the 5000 series. The tang is necked down and threaded to a 5 × 0.9 mm. This is a non-standard size and information about it has not been found.

SHARPENING STONES

Sharpening stones found with SOG knives are of two types. The first is a two-part stone composed of light greenish-grey fine grit and a darker grey grit. In the photo (below right), the small stone is from a seven-inch CISO SOG and is quite rare. It is smaller than the others and was designed to fit in the pocket on that sheath. It is the same color as that found in the other CISO SOG knife sheaths, i.e., a light and dark greenish-grey. When the six-inch pattern came along the stone size was increased. The middle stone is found in the CISO and Presentation sheaths. It was most likely made by Matsunaga Stone Co. of Japan. An example of a similar stone still in the box is shown below. The stone at the right is a two-part stone composed of tan and brown grit. This stone is typically found in the Iron Guard sheaths.

This information may be helpful in determining if a knife is correct or otherwise. Wonderful examples of six-inch blue-bladed SOG knives that have been made one at a time by custom knife makers have been observed. Often, the maker duplicated the knife as a tribute to the men who carried them, but once the knife left their possession it is easy for a dishonest dealer to try to pass it off as an original SOG knife. In evaluating a knife, it pays to look beyond the blade. You may find the handle is dark from use and the sheath bears wrinkles, and may have been re-dyed and waxed all in an attempt to make it match a new knife. Look at the knife and sheath as a package and they should show equal and consistent wear.

STONE POCKET FLAP ATTACHMENTS

One final bit of information about sheaths is how the flaps of the stone pockets are attached. The seven-inch has a single line of stitching across the flap at the throat of the pocket. The CISO six-inch sheath is stitched in a square and then riveted in the center. The Presentation sheath has a single line of stitching and then a rivet. The Iron Guard sheath is held below the sheath throat with two small rivets.

COUNTERFEITS, FAKES, AND COPIES

A word about fakes and counterfeits: the knife in the photograph below, along with the sheath, is a copy the author made some years ago. In making this, there was no intention to fool anyone; it should be pointed out that as the value of authentic pieces increases, so does the likelihood there is somebody who will attempt to profit from a collector

who can not identify with certainty what it is they are looking at, so it pays to do your homework and learn what it is you should look for when examining a potential purchase. Copies have been made for many purposes—mostly legitimate—but copies change hands and not all those who acquire them have honest objectives. The six-inch knife and sheath shown (below left) is a commercial copy of the Sterile Iron Guard and Presentation sheath made in India in the mid-1980s and sold by Atlanta Cutlery Company. These were to provide those who wanted an example but could not afford an original the opportunity to have a look-alike. The sheath is a strong indicator it is a copy, in that the rivets are a two-piece copper harness. The pommel was marked "India" and the ricasso was stamped "M.R.L./Conyers, GA/Mfg 1985." M.R.L. stands for Museum Replicas Limited. These are often doctored and offered as genuine SOG knives.

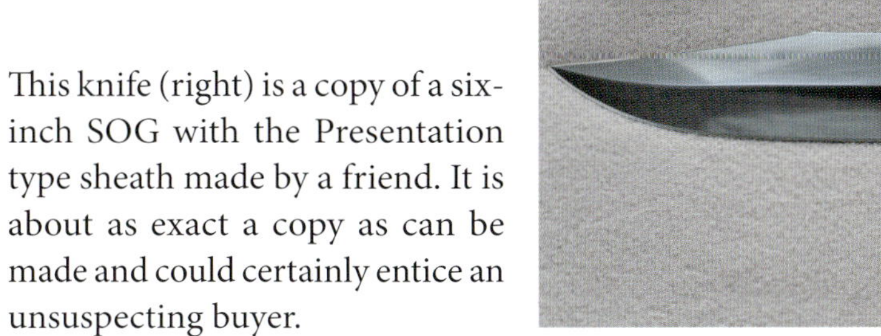

This knife (right) is a copy of a six-inch SOG with the Presentation type sheath made by a friend. It is about as exact a copy as can be made and could certainly entice an unsuspecting buyer.

PRESENTATION PIECES, BOLOS, AND BUFFALO BILLS

CISO provided SOG with bolos for use in cutting through the jungle. Some of these were dressed up with chrome or nickel plating, then engraved with a presentation and given as a keepsake to those who were completing a tour of duty. Likewise, other knives were made expressly for presentation, such as the Buffalo Bill knives. These knives had a large bowie-shaped blade and a handle of native hardwood. Like the bolos, they were dressed up with bright plating and engraving. Often distinctive unit insignia were applied to the blade to enhance their appearance. The stiletto shown below is a well made Fairbairn-Sykes style knife in a locally made presentation case. Project Delta was a special reconnaissance unit established in Nha Trang in 1964. It consisted of six recon hunter-killer teams made up of US and RVN Special Forces personnel and was designated Detachment B-52, 5th Special Forces Group.

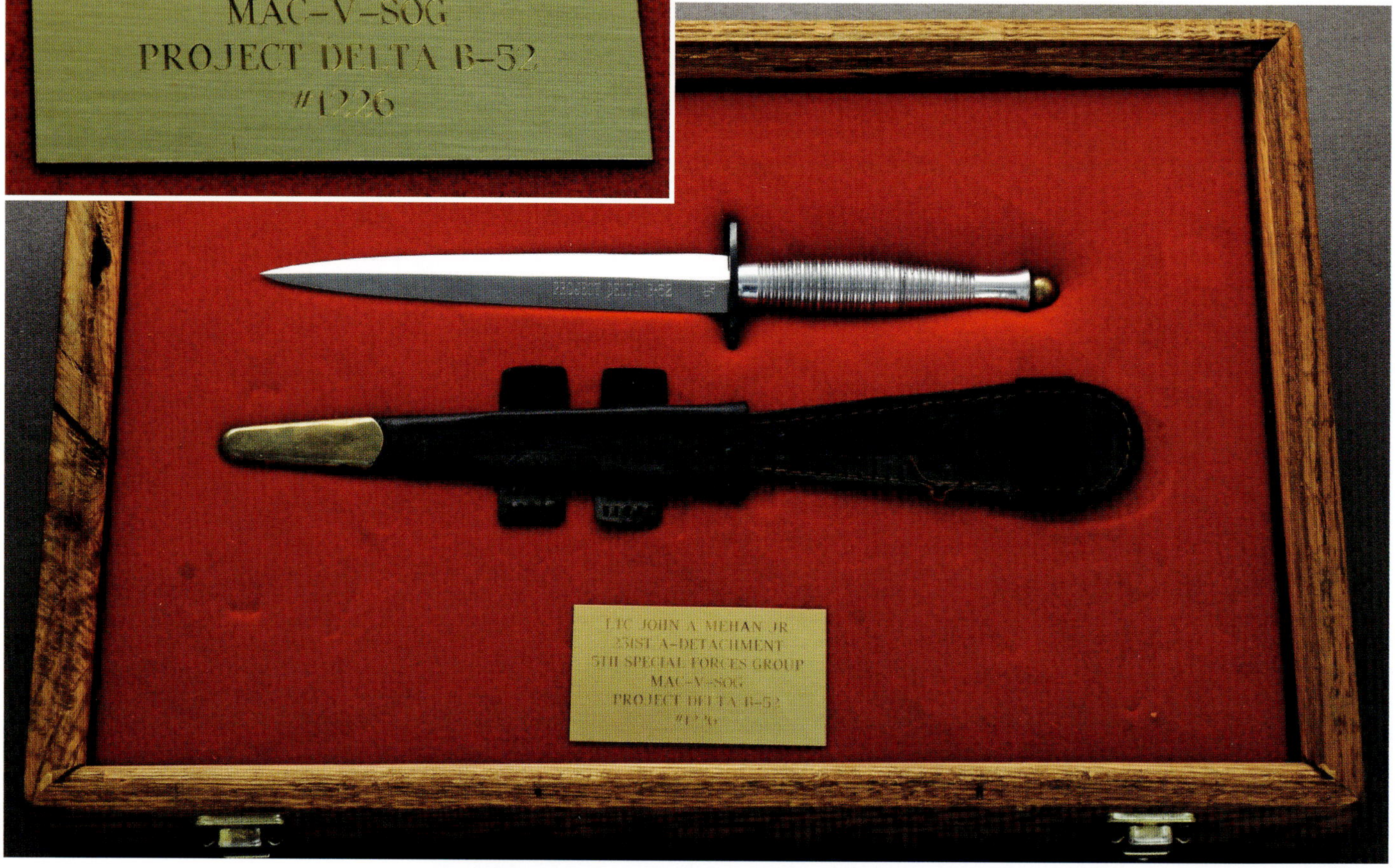

Another presentation stiletto, this one from Mobile Launch Team Two, CCN Da Nang, numbered 1157.

Major Ralph Gilmore spent two tours in Vietnam and was presented with this bolo. He also received two presentation SOG knives shown earlier in this volume.

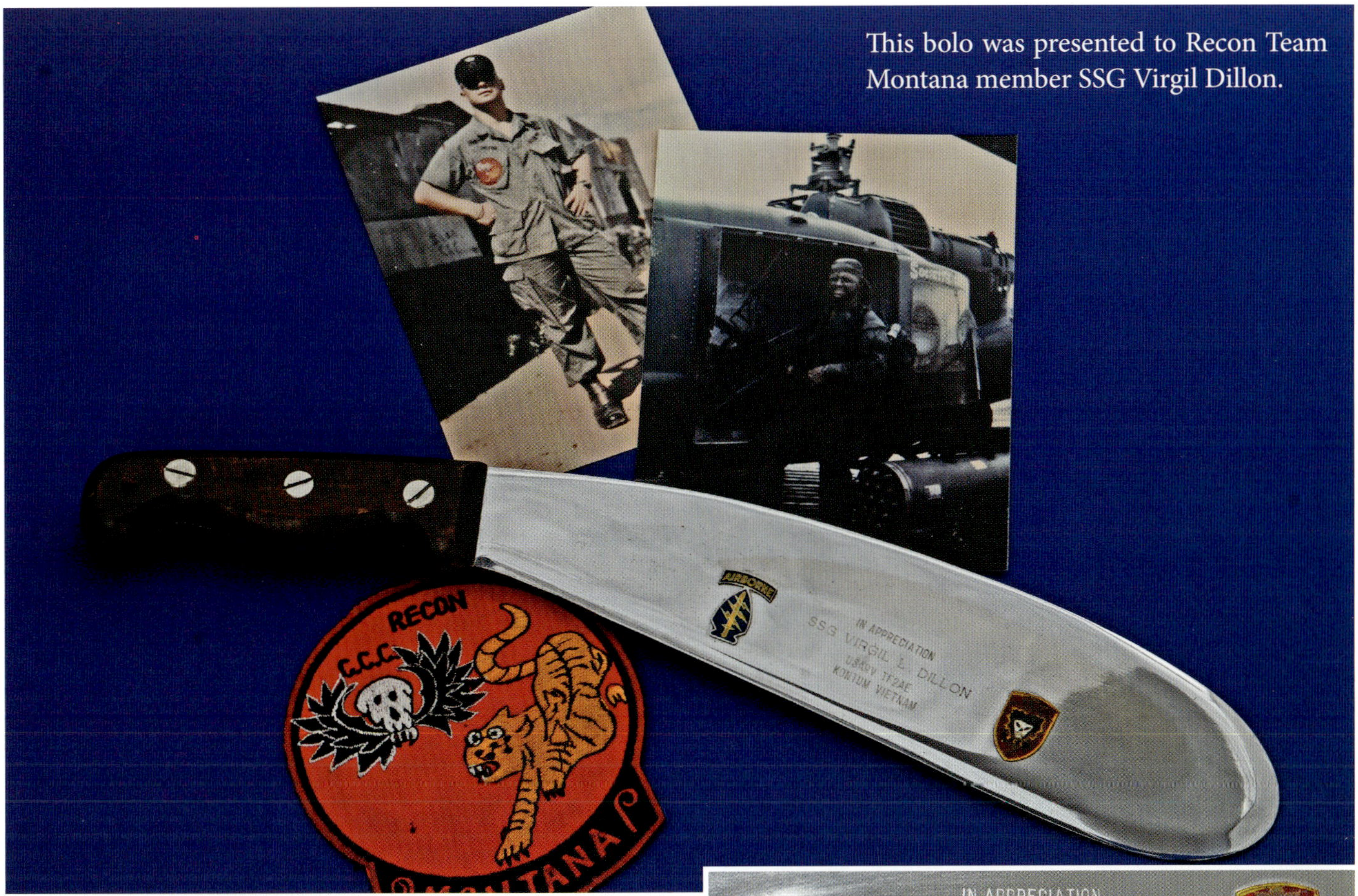

This bolo was presented to Recon Team Montana member SSG Virgil Dillon.

1st Lt. Steven Hatch (left)—a member of Recon Team Kentucky—was the recipient of this bolo.

Personnel photographs courtesy of Jason Hardy, SpecialForcesHistory.com

THE BUFFALO BILL KNIFE

Buffalo Bill Knives were never intended to be used except as presentation pieces. The knife (opposite) is inscribed "SGM CHARLES T. REMAGEN/JUN 67 - JAN 68/HOUSE 10" and displays the unauthorized but well-known SOG insignia. House 10 was a safe house and SOG motor pool in the Chinese area of Saigon. The knife above is inscribed to "SFC HORTON O. DANIELS/HQ MACV - SOG/ VIETNAM FEB 71 - NOV 71."

This presentation is not personalized, but does express someone's disdain for "Shining Brass," an operation in which MACV-SOG was authorized to begin cross border operations into Laos to recon the Ho Chi Minh Trail. The operations were quite risky, and made worse because they were fraught with politics, making it nearly impossible to accomplish anything.

This knife belonged to George Washington Lampkin Sr., who was born in Texas in 1928. He served twenty-eight years in the United States Army, including two tours in Vietnam. At the completion of his tour in December 1968, he was presented with this Buffalo Bill knife by the men of MACV-SOG. OP-35 was the fifth section of SOG and represented ground operations, including reconnaissance behind enemy lines. Many recon teams consisting of US and Vietnamese soldiers were sent into Laos, Cambodia, and North Vietnam, conducting missions there. They were there without identification or uniforms, and there would be no acknowledgment of their activities. At unbelievable risk they operated amidst the enemy, gathering intelligence beyond the support of conventional military. If these teams got into trouble there would be no artillery, tanks, nor air support. They were on their own to find a way out of it. Some teams went in and were never heard from again. SOG was staffed by the army, air force, navy, and marine corps personnel, but it was the Army Special Forces who provided most of the men.

The Buffalo Bill knife shown below was presented to Master Sgt. Morris G. Worley. The term "Ground Studies Group" is another name for OP-35, the umbrella organization for the multitude of recon teams that operated throughout southeast Asia. Most of the recon teams were led by American Special Forces—Green Berets.

This round tip bolo originated with CISO. Occasionally one would be dressed up and given as a presentation. This one reads "IN APPRECIATION/ SGT KEITH E. PLANCICH/SOA (CCC) 5TH SFGA/KNOTUM, VIETNAM." The plaque reads, "PRESENTED TO GREEN BERET/SGT KEITH E. PLANCICH/532-50-2990/5TH SPECIAL FORCES GROUP AIRBORNE/1ST SPECIAL FORCES,/REPUBLIC OF VIETNAM/1970 - 71."

This presentation bolo is etched, "IN APPRECIATION/ SFC RICHARD E. GROSS/SOA (CCC) 5TH SFGA/ KONTUM, VIETNAM." These bolos were rough tools designed for hard use, but those shown have been cleaned up and polished as presentation gifts.

The Western W49—readily available in the PX—was often the artist's canvas for a presentation award.

MACV-SOG was a fairly small unit. In 1969, SOG was authorized 394 personnel. Operational units included another 1,500 military and CIA personnel. If you add in non-US civilian and military personnel, the total assigned to or working for MACV-SOG exceeds 10,000. The knives were distributed far and wide within this group, and many were used up in the jungle; of the thousands of knives issued, relatively few exist in collections today. From time to time new specimens do surface. Occasionally, we are able to add to our collections and our knowledge by purchasing from or trading with the original recipients or other collectors.

OTHER RELATED KNIVES

There are other blades associated with MACV-SOG and special forces, but they do not fall into the typical SOG knife description. SOG was staffed by the navy, marines, air force, and army, with the bulk of the US force being US Army Special Forces. For the collector, there is always some lack of clarity understanding the difference between SOG and the USFS, particularly when some men served under both commands. Most of these men were professional soldiers and some brought to battle their own knives and other personal equipment. Special forces, like SOG, received support and assistance from CISO, and you will find quite a bit of crossover of equipment and such, so in this section we will see some of the knives men were issued, carried, or even purchased to use, or to take home as souvenirs. Most are what you might expect serious soldiers to carry into war, but some are just for looks. There were hundreds of knives in use and available to the servicemen in Vietnam. What will be shown are some of the more rare or unique knives that came out of the war.

THE TALLMAN PUSH DAGGER

The Tallman Knife. These were made at the direction of the CIA in Japan in some numbers, probably in the early 1960s. The name derives from the man who designed or had them made. I am not sure if the spelling of the name is correct. The handle is a synthetic material, perhaps Pakkawood, and is held in place with a single rivet. The overall measurement is 8 inches and the blade is 5.5 inches long. The scabbard is leather and can be attached to wrist or ankle with the straps provided. The handle fits the palm and the fingers go over the guard; it is used like a push dagger. The one shown on the red background belongs to Ben Baker, who acquired it from an agency employee in Okinawa. I know of one other specimen that exist in a private collection.

Another knife in the Ben Baker collection is this dive knife prototype of his design. A very small number of these—about forty—were made for SOG. This is the only one known to remain.

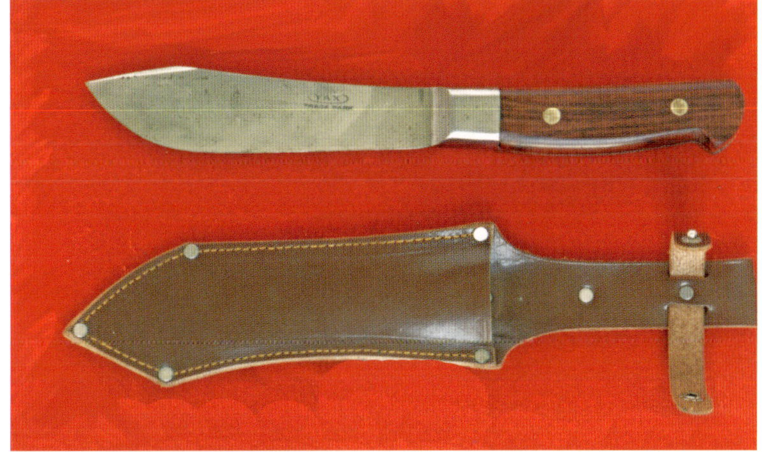

This knife came to Ben Baker by way of being a supply item of the CIA in the early 1960s. It is by the Japanese maker YAX. It is a well made stainless steel knife with hardwood handle scales.

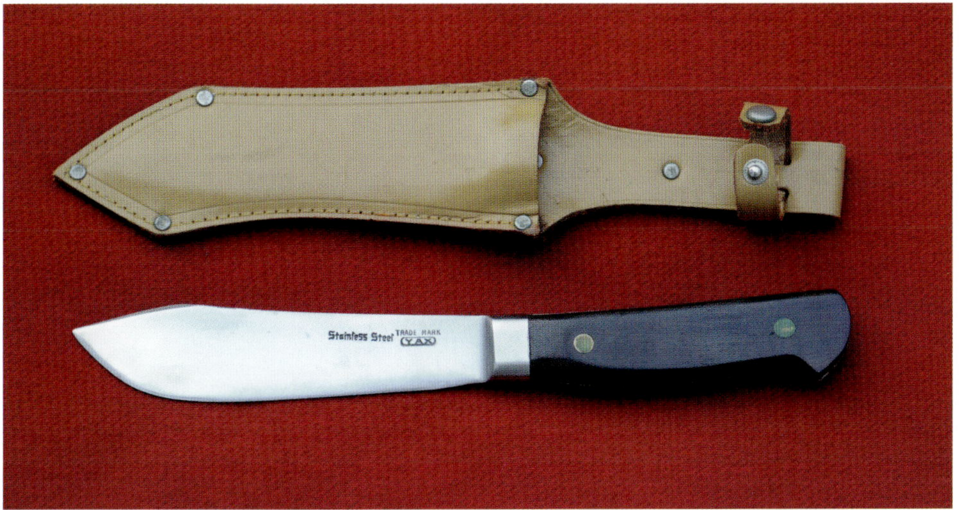

Adjacent is another variation of the YAX knife. This hunter/utility pattern knife is made from forged stainless steel with an integral bolster and hardwood handle.

RELATED KNIVES

This is not a SOG knife, but there is an obvious similarity of the cast iron fittings and those on the iron guard SOG model. This knife is marked "KIFFE/JAPAN" and is one of a few variations of the knife: another has a rounded pommel and smooth handle, while another has white spacers after the first and prior to the final leather washer in the handle. The knife is inexpensively made and has a rather thin blade compared to the SOG knives. This knife was once known to collectors as the Marine Recon Knife, but time has shown these were commercially available. The sheath is rather flimsy and usually did not survive the knife. The beret and photos above are of Lt. Robert Brown, who was the officer in charge of River Section 525.

The fittings on the above knife are identical to those found on the standard Sterile Iron Guard SOG model.

The Western Bowie Knife was a large well made knife available in the PX. The above knife is marked, "MAJ HAROLD E JOHNSON 091887/CO B 5TH SFG (ABN) 1ST SF/26 MAR 67 - 12 JUN 67/PLEIKU RVN" and the knife to the left is marked, "CO B 5TH SFG (ABN) 1ST SF/MAJ WILLIAM C DUKES 077371/ 14 MAR 67 - 24 JUL 67/ PLEIKU, VIETNAM." Most of these were presented to officers with relatively short periods of service and all were out of Pleiku, Vietnam.

Thousands of these round-tipped bolos were supplied by CISO to US and indigenous personnel, and they were favorites for use as presentation pieces. The metal was polished or plated and the wood was darkened before the presentation was etched on the blade. The folding knife is known as the C-4 knife, as it is designed for dealing with C-4 and other explosives. The knife possessing a non-sparking blade of beryllium copper was made by Camillus Cutlery Company for the military. Some 150 of these were sent to Vietnam in 1968, to be tested in the field, and the project ended without a contract for additional knives. In total, less than 200 of these were ever made.

PRESENTED TO
MSG WILLIAM H. JONES
ASST LOG SGT, 29th GEN SPT GP
LONG BINH, RVN
1971 - 1972

Presentation plaques were popular gifts for personnel rotating back to the states at the end of their tours of duty. Many of these plaques (above) centered around a knife. In this case a bolo, but other knives—bayonets, SOGs, and stilettos—have been observed. The Western W49 Bowie (below) was a familiar item in the Post Exchange and many ended up as souvenirs or were given as mementos of service to men headed home. Similarly, plaques depicting a graphic image of the unit insignia in painted brass were made in local trophy shops and were given with an engraved brass plate. Some depicted the crossed flags of South Vietnam and the United States.

The Western Cutlery Company of Boulder, Colorado, made a good quality large, nine and one-half inch blade Bowie knife. These were available with a few options. One came with an imitation stag handle as opposed to the standard rosewood version. A presentation wall plaque was also available. These were sold in ample quantities and many ended up as souvenirs or presentation awards, probably due to the fact that they were widely available and were of an impressive size.

More than 10,000 of these square-tip bolos (above) were provided by the Counter Insurgency Support Office. The scabbard was aluminum clad wood and the blade was laminated steel with two soft layers on each side of a hardened center layer. It was an effective tool, but was heavy and tended to make unwanted noise while moving through the jungle as it rattled in the scabbard.

Special forces purchased a large number of these presentation stilettos to be used to honor men, particularly at the end of a tour of duty. The blade was engraved, "5th Special Forces Group/Vietnam." The cross guard was stamped with the special forces insignia. These low quality, bright-plated knives were made by Japan Sword.

This knife (above) is one of several made by a local blade smith in Nha Trang, Vietnam, for members of the 5th Special Forces Group. The blade is dated 1965. The scabbard is also locally made and of good quality leather. The hardwood handle is stamped "Vietnam 5th S.F." on one side and "De Opresso Liber" on the other side. This is a typical native-made knife. It is fabricated from materials like scrap aluminum, brass, or spring steel reshaped and repurposed as a knife blade. The handle is locally grown hardwood. The leather is water buffalo hide. Knife researcher and author Frank Trzaska notes that US advisors in Vietnam often carried these because it assisted their acceptance by the local natives. The large knife at the left is a locally made presentation piece ready for an inscription.

The knives shown below are typical of those made by the native Montagnard tribesmen. These were made in KonTum, which is in the central highlands of Vietnam, near the borders of Laos and Cambodia. The floral decorations on the blades are typical and were usually made by the application of only one or two different punches. The punch also imprinted the city name or initials on the front side of the blades and "Vietnam" or "V-N" on the reverse. The sheaths, identical in design, must have come out of the same shop, but one is top grain leather, while the other still bears the fur of the original critter—probably a pot belly pig.

This large Bowie knife is made from ¼ inch stock and is quite stout. It has a full tang covered with walnut scales held in place with three rivets. The blade is ten inches long. This came out of a special operations warehouse at Ton Son Nhut Air Base just outside Saigon. It was carried by an NCO who used it as a machete. It did not have a sheath when he received it so he had one made locally. The sheath is quite typical of those from that area. I have seen several over the years that must have been made in the same shop.

NGUYEN DAN KNIVES

The 1990 winter issue of *Knives Illustrated* contained an article by Bob Worthington titled, "Vietnam's Own Combat Knives." Worthington was a senior advisor to an infantry regiment of the Army of the Republic of Vietnam, and while at the Lam Son National Training Center he heard about a blade smith in the nearby central coastal village Ninh Hoa. The smith was Nguyen Dan, and he made remarkable knives under the most primitive conditions. He used discarded jeep or auto steel springs for his blades. He would hand-forge these into rough rectangular blanks later to be forged and shaped into blades. The guards were made of expended brass small arms shell casings melted and cast into oval guards. The handles were from local water buffalo horn. The knives are substantial, with blades of ¼ inch steel and brass guards of the same thickness. Handles had finger grooves and were large. The design was simple.

These are fairly typical of what Nguyen Dan made, but other shapes have been observed. Even one in the distinctive shape of a seven-inch SOG recon has been seen. His quality control was admirable. After the final tempering he would slap and beat the blade against the anvil to see if it was too brittle. If it passed this test without breaking or bending it went on to final assembly. Then the finished knife had to shave metal from a rod that hung in his shop. After that it had to shave hair. If it could do that it was ready to go. His knives are among the best combat knives found anywhere in the world.

This large Nguyen Dan combat knife is shown with its sheath, which is somewhat typical, but a variety of sheaths have been observed, including some made from the hide of pot belly pigs with hair remaining on the top grain.

This fine blade records a soldier's place and dates of service and makes a great memento, as well as a combat knife.

RANDALL MADE KNIVES

Randall Made Knives are legendary. They have been carried by our servicemen since WWII and continue to be prized today. It is sometimes quipped that a special forces soldier can be recognized by his Rolex watch and his Randall knife. These handmade knives are known for their functional and beautiful designs and for their expert fit and finish, particularly those with handles of natural materials like stag, wood, and leather. Randall Knives make a variety of models for hunters, fishermen, firemen, and many others, each specifically tailored to a particular job. They also make a number of models for soldiers, and we will look at a few of those. The model shown below dates from the late 1940s or early 1950s. It is a Model 1, dubbed the "All Purpose Fighting Knife," and sports a Model 2 style handle of stacked leather washers. The blade is eight inches long.

This knife is a Model 1 Randall with a Sambar Stag handle with finger grooves. The knife has an eight-inch blade. Its design and construction are typical of those knives made by Randall during the Vietnam War era.

This knife is a Randall #1 with a black Micarta handle with finger grooves and a seven inch blade. Knives made during this period equipped with a stacked leather washer were done with five-colored spacers of vulcanized fiber between the handle and guard. Those with non-leather handles like this one were dressed out in seven spacers. The knife on the following page is the quintessential Randall fighting knife, recognized at a glance around the world by professional soldiers. Its classic shape and fine lines, along with its stacked leather handle, are key identifiers. This one is somewhat unusual, in that it has a pommel of brass rather than the standard aluminum.

Another Randall Model 1, but this one sports a handsome ivory handle. It makes a fine package indeed with its brown button sheath. Made prior to 1962. The Models 1 and 2 shown on the next page both have black Micarta handles, but what makes them special is their special order riveted sheaths.

These Randall Model 2 (left) and Model 1 (right), with their stacked leather washer handles, are typical of those made during the mid-1960s.

Many a soldier repurposed his old hunting knife when assigned to a combat zone. In this case it was a Randall Model 4 with a very nice finger groove handle of Sambar stag with seven spacers. The blade is six inches long and is shown with its original brown button sheath.

Sometime after World War II, Randall decided to make a heavy duty combat knife and the Model 14 came to life. The first of these came with handles of Tenite, a plastic developed in 1929. Most were green, but they did try other colors as well. The material was not dimensionally stable and it gave way after a short time to Micarta. Most of these Tenite 14s had an exposed tang. These early knives are much favored by collectors.

Here is another early Randall 14 with a green Tenite handle. These early models came with sheaths equipped with a keeper strap held in place with a canteen snap.